STICKY FINGERS

DINOSAURS

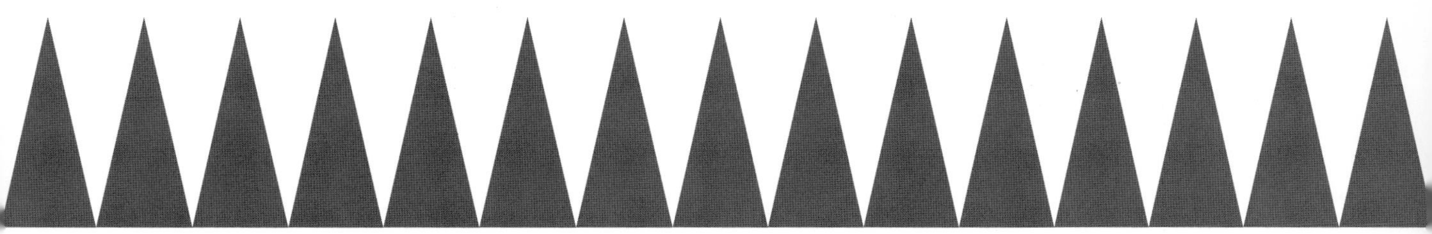

Ting and Neil Morris

Illustrated by Ruth Levy and Joanne Cowne

SEA-TO-SEA
Mankato Collingwood London

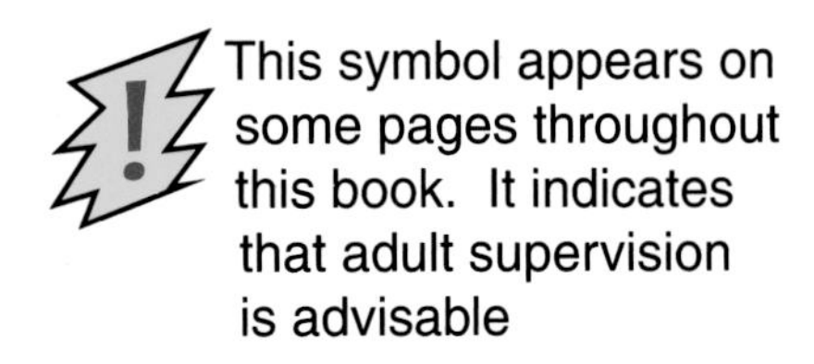

This symbol appears on some pages throughout this book. It indicates that adult supervision is advisable

This edition first published in 2007 by
Sea-to-Sea Publications
1980 Lookout Drive
North Mankato
Minnesota 56003

Printed in China

Library of Congress Cataloging-in-Publication Data
Morris, Ting.
Dinosaurs / by Ting and Neil Morris (authors) ; Ruth Levy and Joanne Cowne (illustrators).
p. cm. -- (Sticky fingers)
Includes bibliographical references and index.
Summary: Provides step-by-step instructions for such dinosaur crafts as a tyrannosaurus hobby horse, plaster casts of dinosaur feet, and a flying pterodactyl.
ISBN-13: 978-1-59771-029-9
1. Handicraft--Juvenile literature. 2. Modeling--Juvenile literature. 3. Papercraft--Juvenile literature. 4. Paleontology--Juvenile literature. 5. Dinosaurs--Juvenile literature. I. Morris, Neil, 1946- II. Levy, Ruth, ill. III. Cowne, Joanne, ill. IV. Title.

TT160.M639 2006
745.5--dc22

2005058173

9 8 7 6 5 4 3 2

Published by arrangement with the Watts Publishing Group Ltd, London

Editor: Hazel Poole
Consultant: David Lambert
Designer: Sally Boothroyd
Photography: John Butcher
Artwork: Ruth Levy/Joanne Cowne
Models: Emma Morris
Picture research: Ambreen Húsain

Contents

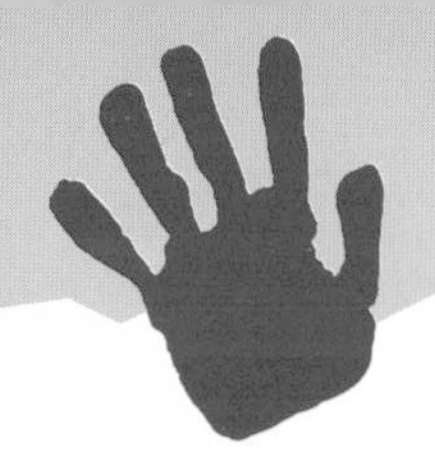

Introduction

In this book you can learn about dinosaurs both by reading about them and by having fun with craft activities. The information in the fact boxes will tell you about the meat-eating dinosaurs and the plant-eaters, as well as related reptiles. Of course, no one has ever seen a dinosaur as humans appeared on Earth over 60 million years after the dinosaurs had died out. So all that we know about them has been learned from fossils — remains preserved in rocks.

At the end of the book is a time chart to show you when all the dinosaurs mentioned in this book lived. There is also a list of places to visit and books to read if you want to find out more.

So get ready to get your fingers sticky — making dinosaurs as you read all about them!

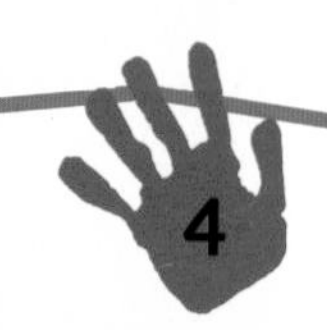

Equipment and Materials

The projects in this book provide an introduction to the use of different art and craft media, and need little adult help. Most of the objects are made with throwaway household "junk" such as boxes, plastic bottles and containers, newspaper, and fabric remnants. Natural things such as seeds, sticks, sand, and stones are also used. Paints, brushes, glues, and modeling materials will have to be bought, but if stored correctly will last for a long time and for many more craft activities.

In this book the following materials are used:

air-hardening modeling clay
balloon (round)
broom handle
brushes (for glue and paint)
buttons
canes (pencil thickness, for gardening)
cardboard
cardboard boxes (two must be identical)
cardboard tubes
cellophane
cereal box
curtain ring
egg cartons
fabric (scraps)
felt pieces (red, green, white, black, orange)
felt-tip pens
food coloring (green)
glue (water-based PVA, which can be used for thickening paint and as a varnish, strong glue for sticking plastic, metal, or fabric)
jar (for mixing paint and paste)
materials from nature (sticks, twigs, leaves, stones, pinecones, seeds)
modeling materials (air-hardeningmodeling clay, modeling clay)
oak tag
paint (powder, ready-mixed, or poster paints; watercolor inks)
paper (thick construction paper, corrugated paper, crêpe paper, tissue paper, newspaper)
pencil
pins (straight)
pipe cleaner
plaster of Paris
plastic bottles
popsicle stick
ribbon
rolling pin
ruler
sand (fine, dry builders'sand)
scissors
shoe polish (tan)
silver foil
sponge
stapler
straws
string
tape (parcel tape), adhesive-backed pads
trays and tubs
varnish (PVA mixed with cold water)
wallpaper paste
water

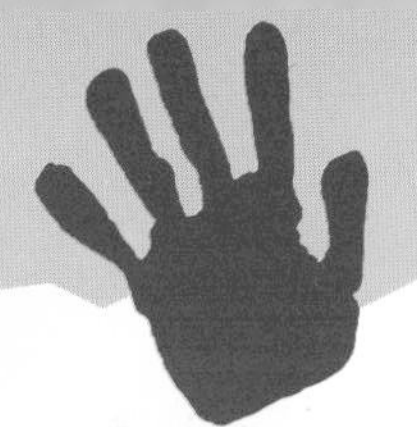

Valley of the Dinosaurs

YOU WILL NEED:
- ✔crêpe paper ✔tissue paper ✔glue
- ✔cellophane ✔modeling clay ✔straws
- ✔shallow box with lid ✔stones and pebbles
- ✔builders' sand ✔colored construction paper
- ✔natural objects (pinecones, twigs, etc.)
- ✔green ink or food coloring

1 To make a prehistoric landscape, first put the shallow box together like this. The lid becomes the background and the base is the valley.

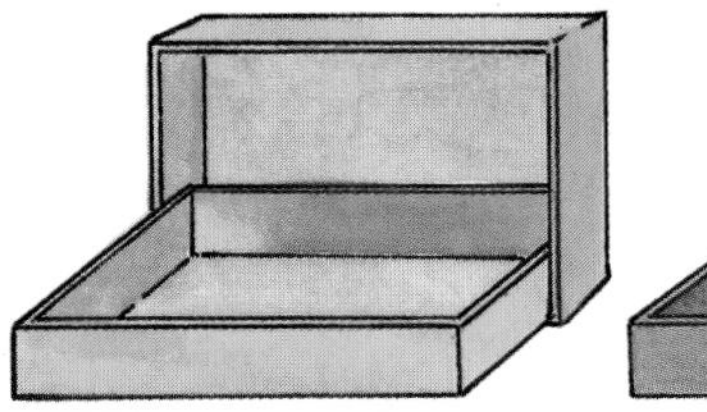

2 Line the box with blue paper. Cut out colored-paper moutains and volcanoes and stick them to the blue sky. The skyline should be above the rim of the box.

3 Color some dry builders' sand green, to make it look like moss. Stir the sand while it is soaking up the coloring.Leave it to dry overnight.

WARNING: Never hold cellophane right up to your face.

4 To make a lake in the valley, lay a piece of blue paper on the base of the box and place some cellophane on top of it. Sprinkle the green sand around the edge.

5 Arrange stones and pebbles to look like mountains with caves and secret passages.

6 Giant trees and plants grow in the valley. Pinecones, twigs, beech husks, and other natural objects pressed into clay trunks make good bushes. Make ferns by taping green tissue paper around straws planted in lumps of clay. Strips of crêpe paper make good creepers.

7 Mold a *Diplodocus* by rolling out a ball of modeling clay and six sausage shapes for a neck, tail, and legs. Press the shapes together and stand the dinosaur up. Mark eyes and mouth with a toothpick. Make lots of other dinosaurs this way and let them roam through the valley of the dinosaurs. (Don't forget that some of the reptiles were as tall as the trees.)

The Age of Reptiles

Dinosaurs were large reptiles. They appeared on Earth about 230 million years ago. The Age of Reptiles lasted for about 165 million years. Then they all died out. But what was the earth like at that time?

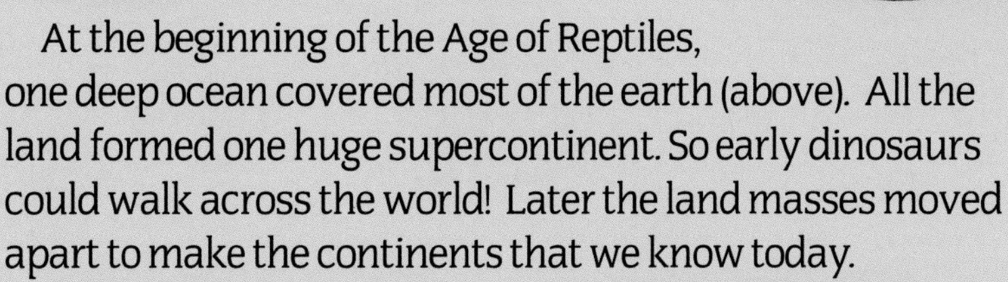

At the beginning of the Age of Reptiles, one deep ocean covered most of the earth (above). All the land formed one huge supercontinent. So early dinosaurs could walk across the world! Later the land masses moved apart to make the continents that we know today.

Fish, amphibians, and giant insects such as dragonflies existed before the dinosaurs. Large fern trees grew in swamps, and there were forests of cone-bearing trees. The first birds and small mammals appeared during the Age of Reptiles, followed later by fruit trees and flowering plants.

Throughout much of their time on earth, dinosaurs probably lived in a tropical climate.

Land near the sea had mild, moist weather all year 'round.

Toward the end of the Age of Reptiles, the climate grew cooler and drier.

Tyrannosaurus Hobbyhorse

YOU WILL NEED:
- ✓*large sock* ✓*pins*
- ✓*broom handle* ✓*ruler*
- ✓*old fabric and newspaper for stuffing*
- ✓*white, black, orange felt*
- ✓*glue* ✓*scissors* ✓*ribbon*

1 Stuff the foot of the sock with scraps of material. Put two small balls of newspaper into the sock to make eye ridges.

2 Cut two 8-in (20 cm) rows of jagged teeth and a strip of red felt 7 x 4 in (18 x 10 cm) for the mouth.

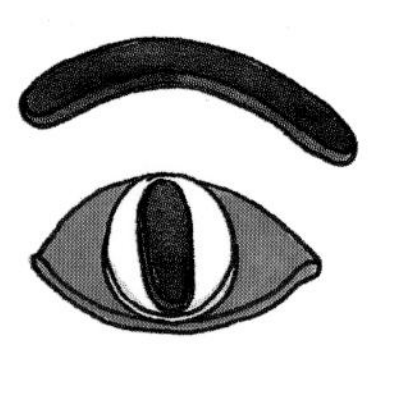

3 Pin the mouth and teeth together before gluing them into position. Remove the pins. Add thin strips of black felt around the mouth as shown.

4 Cut two mean-looking orange felt eyes, two white dots, and black pupils. Assemble the eyes like this. Glue them below the ridges. Cut two black eyebrows and glue them on top of the ridges. Add two red dots for nostrils.

5 Push the broom handle into the sock as far as the heel. Stuff newspaper firmly all around it. Tie a piece of ribbon around the sock to hold the head on. Now you can ride on Tyrannosaurus!

Tyrannosaurus Rex

Tyrannosaurus was the biggest meat-eating dinosaur. It was about 50 ft (15 m) long and weighed between 4 - 7 tons. If this dinosaur were alive today, it would be able to peer into the upstairs windows of a modern house.

Tyrannosaurus fought and often killed other dinosaurs. Some scientists, however, think that it mostly fed on the bodies of dead dinosaurs. This was because it was too slow to catch its own food.

Its head was almost 7 ft (2 m) long, and its long teeth had sawlike edges for tearing flesh. It had powerful claws on its hind legs, which it probably used to grip its prey. But the front legs were very small, with two small fingers on the hand, and could not even reach its mouth.

Tyrannosaurus Rex means "King tyrant lizard."

Dinosaur Footprints

1 Take a ball of clay and make a model dinosaur foot. Gently press it on a flat surface and shape three claws.

YOU WILL NEED:
✔air-hardening modeling clay ✔plaster of Paris ✔modeling clay ✔sponge ✔plastic tray ✔rolling pin ✔construction paper ✔ready-mix paint ✔cloth ✔popsicle stick

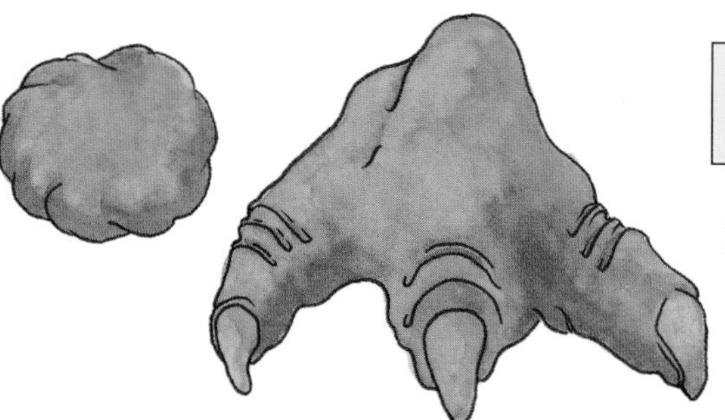

2 Make some marks with a popsicle stick or your finger on the base of the foot. Leave it to harden.

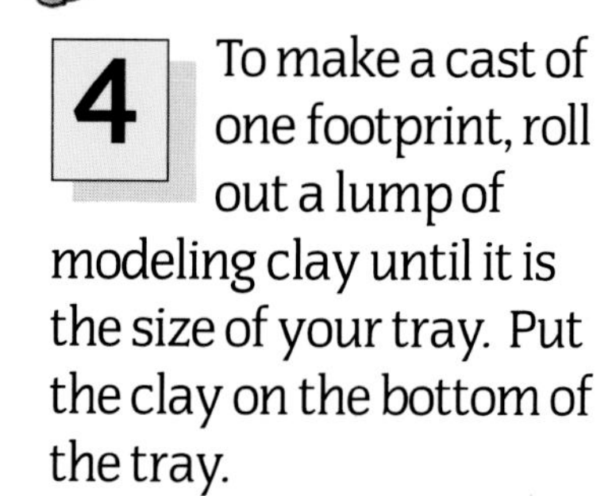

3 Now make a trail of prints across the sheet of paper with your dinosaur foot. Pour some paint onto a sponge and press the foot against it. Print a trail across your paper. Wipe the foot clean if you want to use a different color.

4 To make a cast of one footprint, roll out a lump of modeling clay until it is the size of your tray. Put the clay on the bottom of the tray.

5 Press the foot firmly into the clay and remove it to show a footprint.

6 With an adult's help, mix the plaster of Paris in a bowl with some water. Pour the liquid plaster over the footprint in the clay. You can paint your dinosaur foot while you are waiting for the plaster to dry.

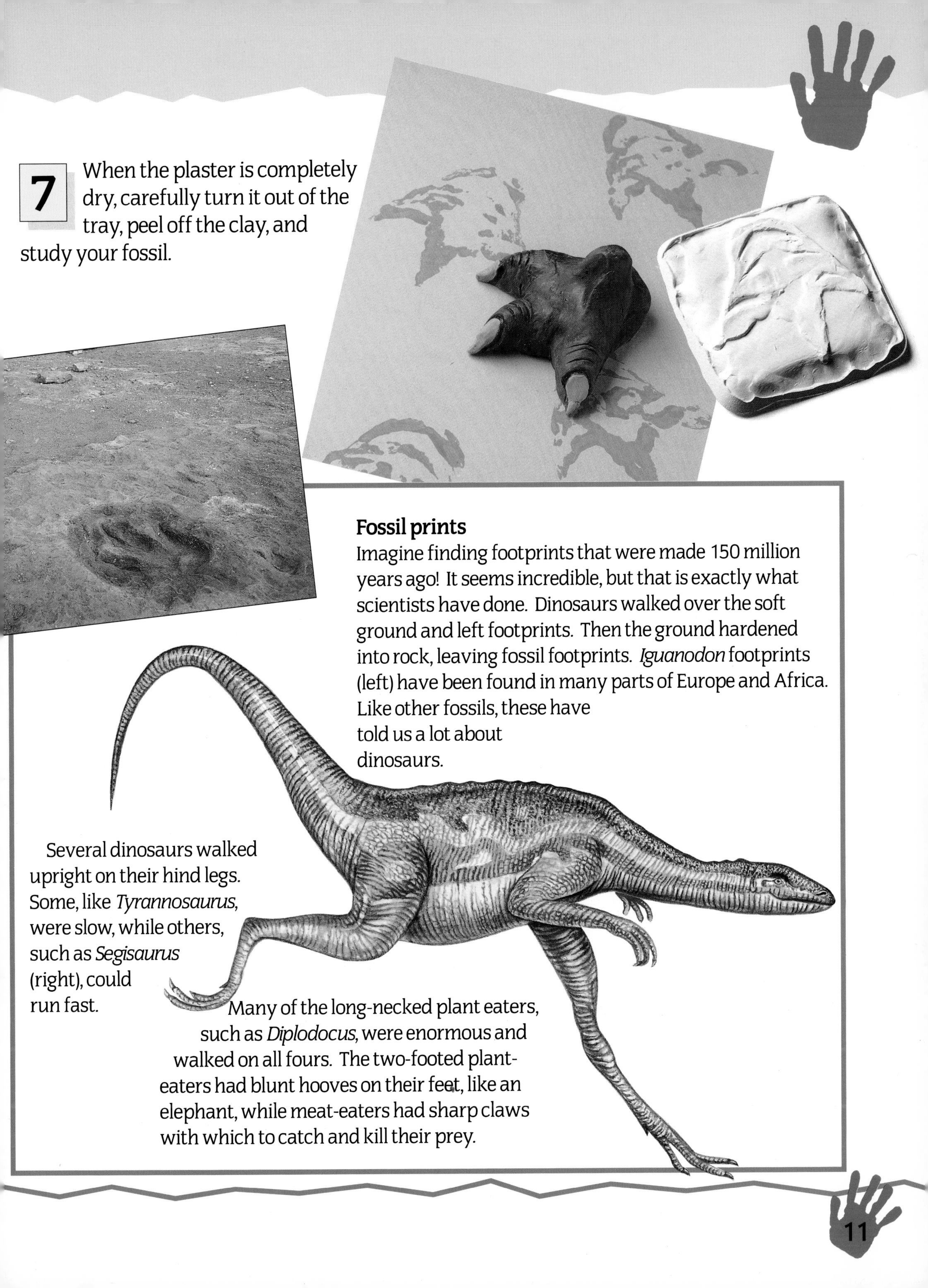

7 When the plaster is completely dry, carefully turn it out of the tray, peel off the clay, and study your fossil.

Fossil prints

Imagine finding footprints that were made 150 million years ago! It seems incredible, but that is exactly what scientists have done. Dinosaurs walked over the soft ground and left footprints. Then the ground hardened into rock, leaving fossil footprints. *Iguanodon* footprints (left) have been found in many parts of Europe and Africa. Like other fossils, these have told us a lot about dinosaurs.

Several dinosaurs walked upright on their hind legs. Some, like *Tyrannosaurus*, were slow, while others, such as *Segisaurus* (right), could run fast.

Many of the long-necked plant eaters, such as *Diplodocus*, were enormous and walked on all fours. The two-footed plant-eaters had blunt hooves on their feet, like an elephant, while meat-eaters had sharp claws with which to catch and kill their prey.

Stegosaurus Disguise

YOU WILL NEED:
✔glue ✔adhesive-backed pads ✔tape ✔ruler
✔scissors ✔egg cartons ✔pencil ✔brushes
✔3 big cardboard boxes (2 must be identical)
✔green construction paper and oak tag ✔pins
✔powder or ready-mix paint ✔silver foil

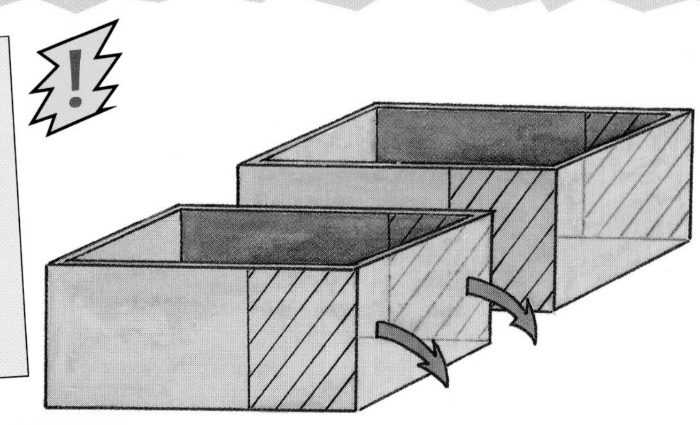

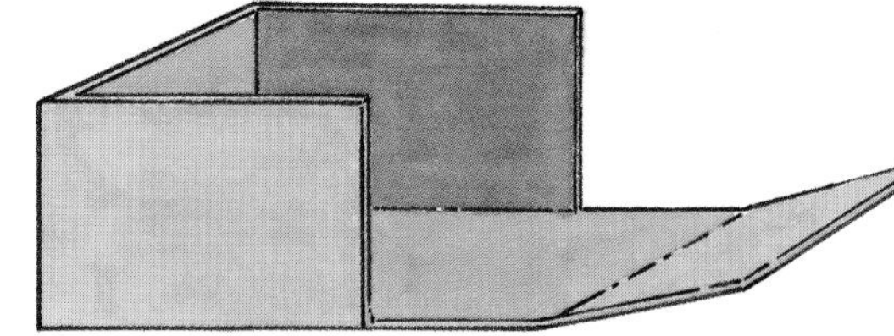

1 Find two identical boxes big enough to fit over your head and shoulders. Ask an adult to cut away the shaded part and open out the bottom of the boxes.

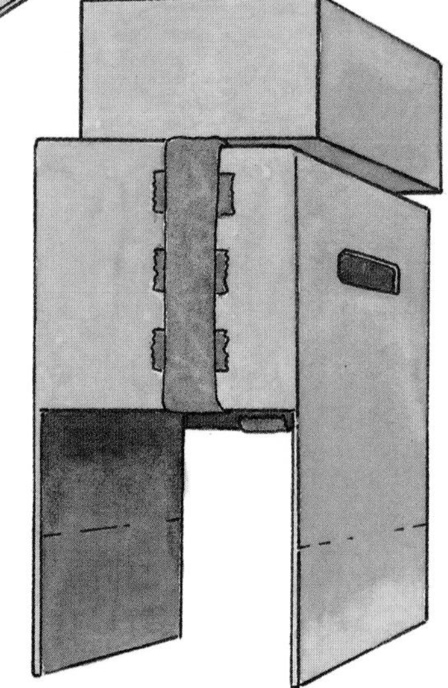

2 Slide one box inside the other and tape them together. Try on your *Stegosaurus* body. Mark the position of your eyes and ask an adult to cut out a peephole in the front.

3 For the head, glue another box on top of the dinosaur body.

4 Now decorate your disguise. Cover the boxes with green paper, or paint them with green paint thickened with PVA glue. When the paint is dry, mark the scales with black paint. Out of construction paper, make two eyes and a mouth with teeth and glue them onto the head.

5 Cut spine plates from oak tag 6 in (15 cm) wide. Add a 1 in (3 cm) fold. Attach the plates to the top of the head box and along the body with adhesive-backed pads under the fold. Secure them with tape.

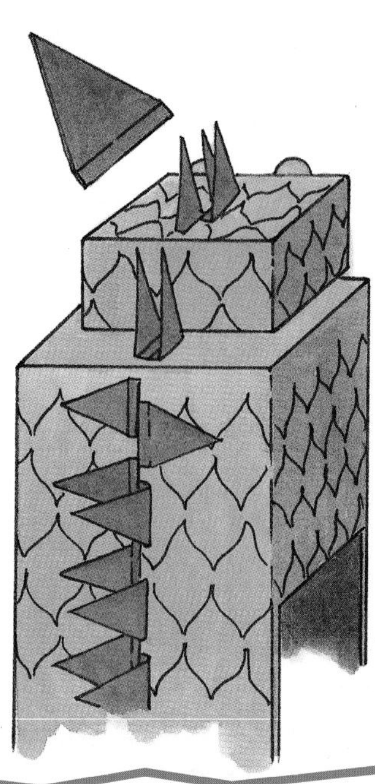

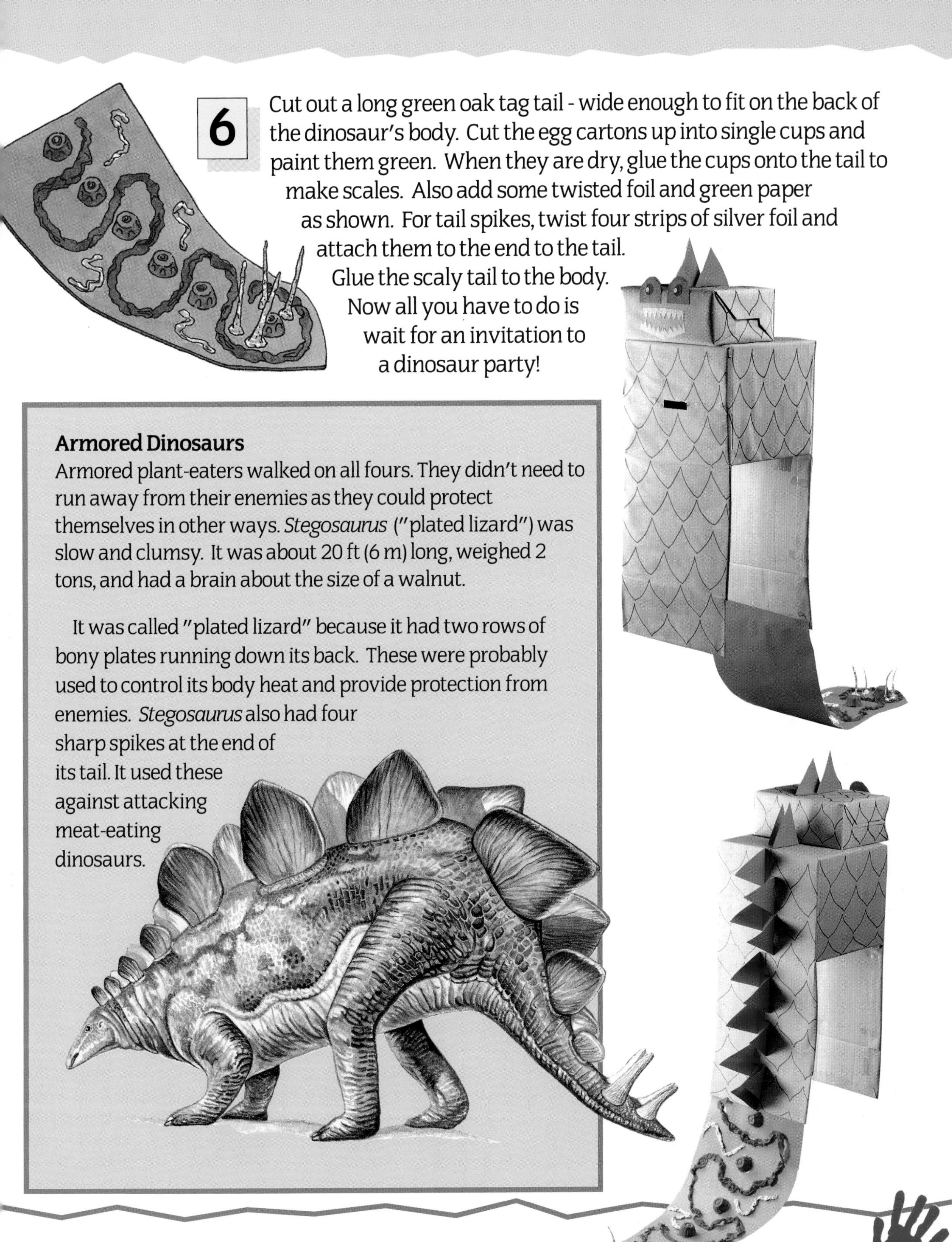

6

Cut out a long green oak tag tail - wide enough to fit on the back of the dinosaur's body. Cut the egg cartons up into single cups and paint them green. When they are dry, glue the cups onto the tail to make scales. Also add some twisted foil and green paper as shown. For tail spikes, twist four strips of silver foil and attach them to the end to the tail. Glue the scaly tail to the body. Now all you have to do is wait for an invitation to a dinosaur party!

Armored Dinosaurs

Armored plant-eaters walked on all fours. They didn't need to run away from their enemies as they could protect themselves in other ways. *Stegosaurus* ("plated lizard") was slow and clumsy. It was about 20 ft (6 m) long, weighed 2 tons, and had a brain about the size of a walnut.

It was called "plated lizard" because it had two rows of bony plates running down its back. These were probably used to control its body heat and provide protection from enemies. *Stegosaurus* also had four sharp spikes at the end of its tail. It used these against attacking meat-eating dinosaurs.

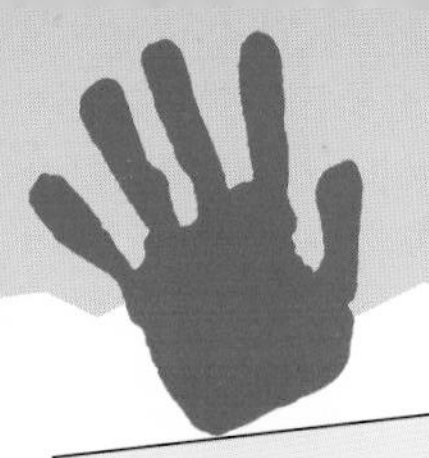

Skeleton

MESSY ACTIVITY

YOU WILL NEED:
✔cardboard ✔straws
✔fine, dry sand ✔scissors
✔PVA glue ✔glue brush

Be a fossil hunter and make your own dinosaur skeleton.

1 Cut up straws into different lengths for bones. Fit the straws together on a cardboard base, copying a drawing of a dinosaur skeleton.

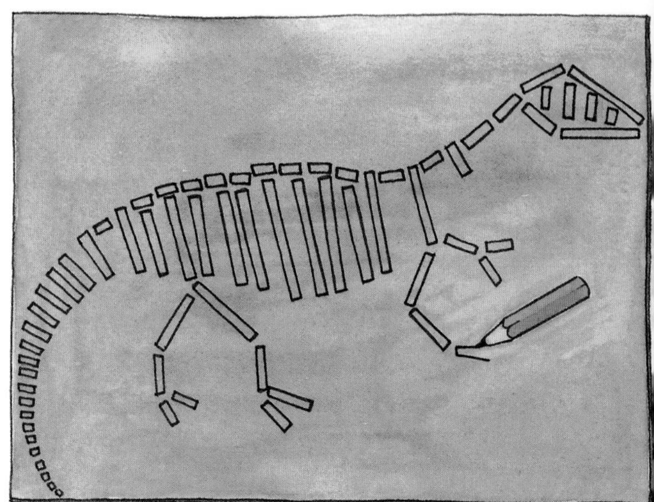

2 When you have assembled the skeleton, glue the straws down one by one. Brush each straw with PVA glue and stick it in position. Make sure that all the straws are firmly attached to the cardboard base. Wait for the glue to dry.

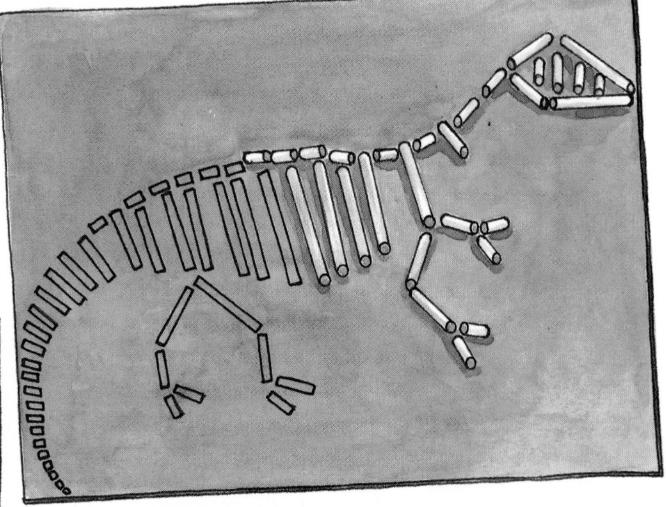

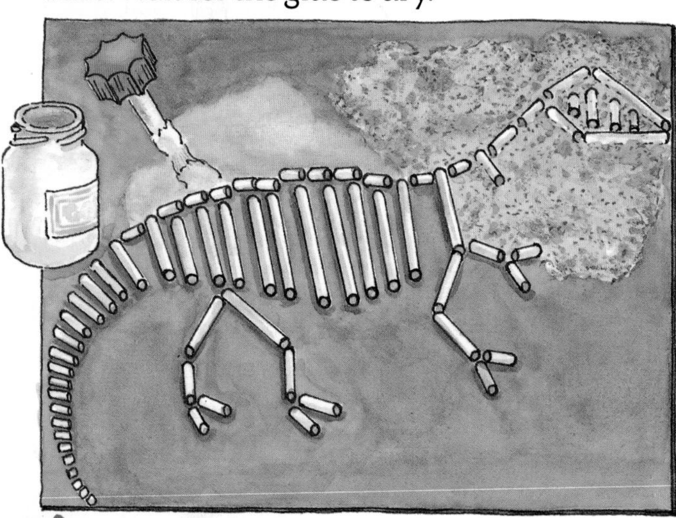

3 Now brush some glue thickly between the bones and all around the straw skeleton. Sprinkle sand over the glue. It is best to work with a small section at a time while the glue is still wet.

Dinosaur Bones

There are many dinosaur skeletons on display in museums. The fossil bones of a complete skeleton are wired together by experts. But it is rare for fossil bones to be neatly arranged when they are found. They are usually broken up in the rocks into small pieces. They have to be put together in the right order to make the animal recognizable.

When Gideon and Mary Mantell found dinosaur remains in 1822, they named the creature *Iguanodon* ("iguana tooth"). This was because the teeth looked like those of the South American iguana lizard.

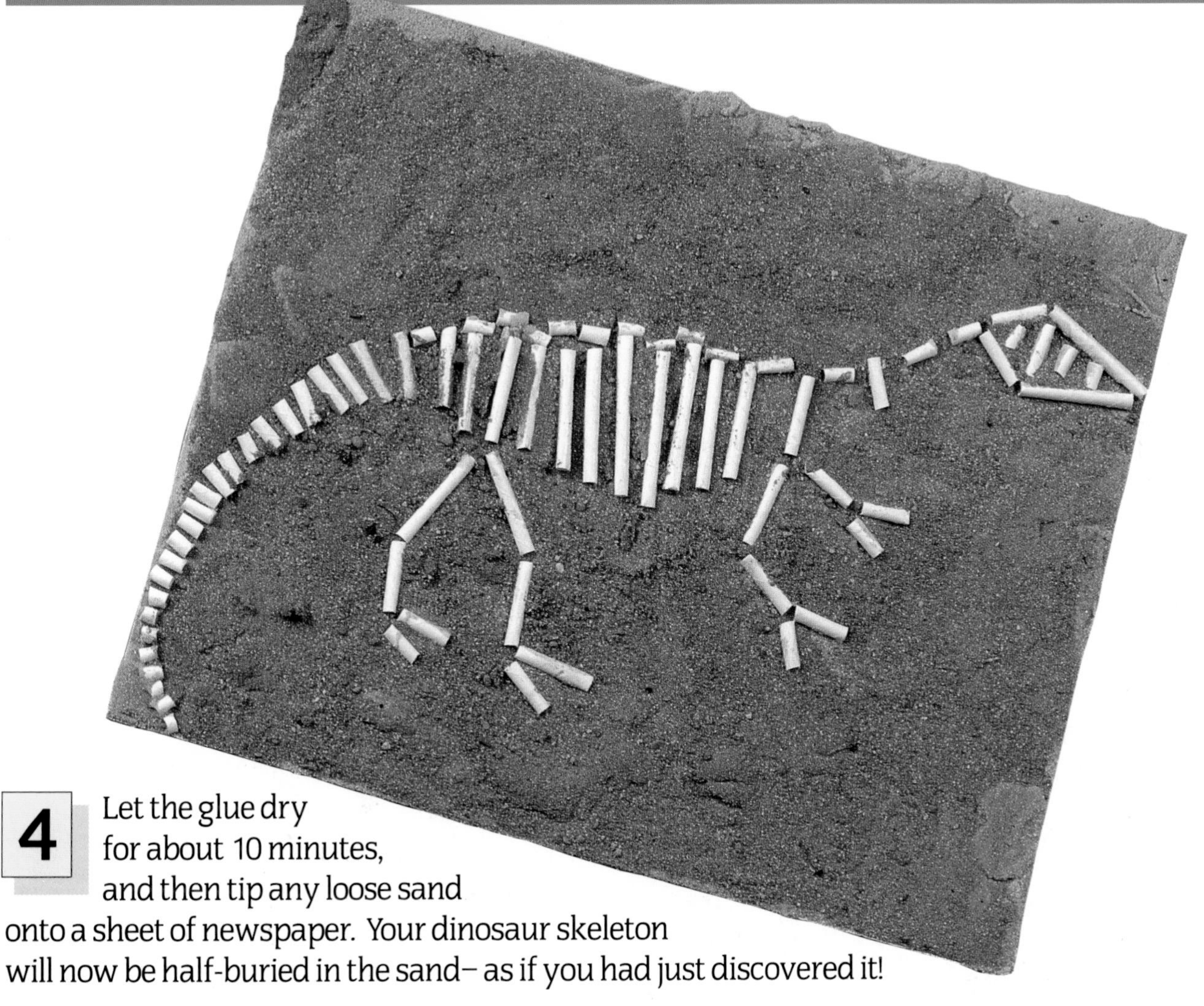

4 Let the glue dry for about 10 minutes, and then tip any loose sand onto a sheet of newspaper. Your dinosaur skeleton will now be half-buried in the sand– as if you had just discovered it!

Flying Reptiles

YOU WILL NEED:
✔colored oak tag or thick paper ✔pipe cleaners ✔nylon thread ✔curtain ring ✔glue brush ✔glue ✔scissors ✔tape ✔black felt-tip pen ✔ruler ✔pencil

1 To make a pet *Pteranodon* fold a piece of oak tag 4 x 11 in (10 x 28 cm) in half lengthwise.

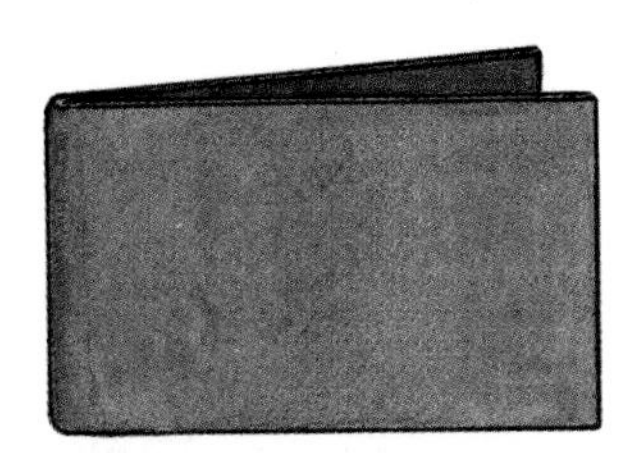

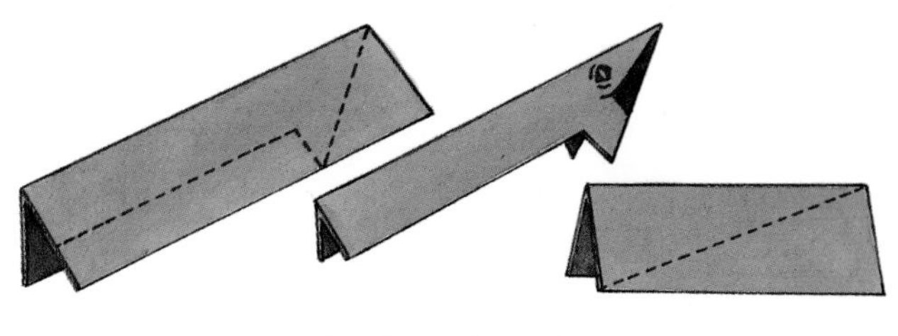

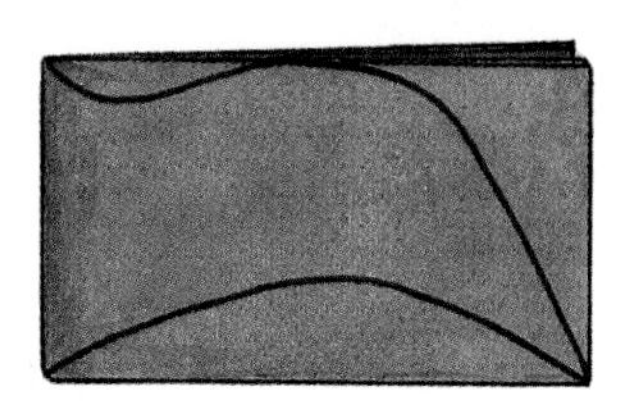

2 Copy the shape of the wing and cut it out. Don't cut the fold.

3 For the head and beak, fold a piece of oak tag 4 x $2\frac{1}{2}$ in (10 x 6 cm) in half lengthwise. Copy this shape and cut it out. Don't cut the fold. Draw the eyes and beak with black felt-tip pen. Fold a 3-in (8 cm) strip of oak tag lengthwise and cut out a thin tail.

4 Make the body by rolling up a sheet of paper, slightly wider than the center of the wings, and glue it together.

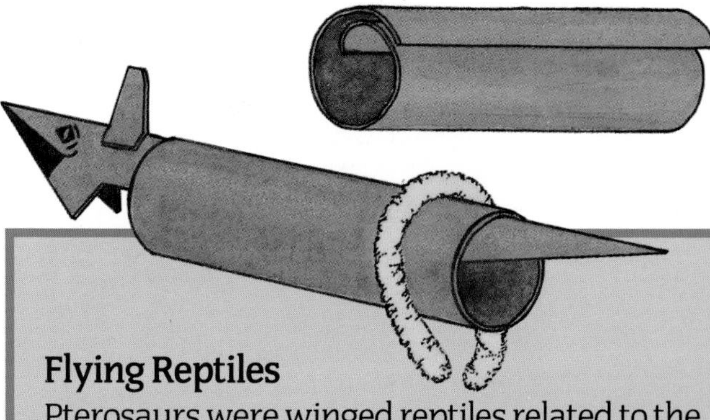

5 Glue pipe cleaner legs at one end of the tube and stick the tail inside the body. Glue on the head. Cut out an oak tag crest and glue it as shown.

6 Open the wings and tape a curtain ring to the wing top.

7 Now glue the wings onto the *Pteranodon's* body.

Flying Reptiles
Pterosaurs were winged reptiles related to the dinosaurs. Their wings were covered with skin and were used for gliding. *Pteranodon* is one of the largest known flying animals that has ever lived. It had a wingspan of 23 ft (7 m). Scientists think that *Pteranodon* lived on high cliffs where it could take off easily. It must have been very clumsy on the ground because it had weak legs and could not fold its wings completely.

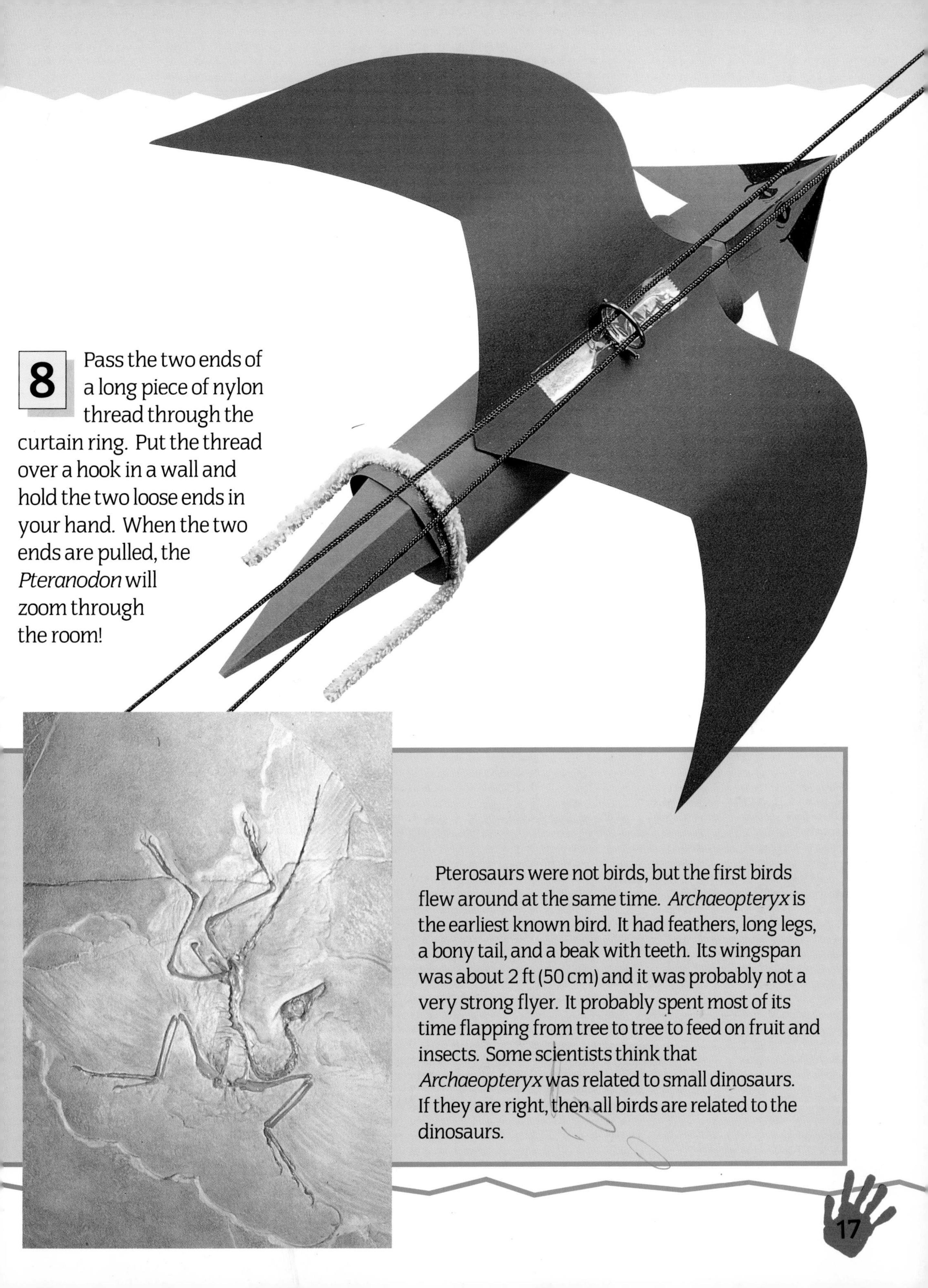

8 Pass the two ends of a long piece of nylon thread through the curtain ring. Put the thread over a hook in a wall and hold the two loose ends in your hand. When the two ends are pulled, the *Pteranodon* will zoom through the room!

Pterosaurs were not birds, but the first birds flew around at the same time. *Archaeopteryx* is the earliest known bird. It had feathers, long legs, a bony tail, and a beak with teeth. Its wingspan was about 2 ft (50 cm) and it was probably not a very strong flyer. It probably spent most of its time flapping from tree to tree to feed on fruit and insects. Some scientists think that *Archaeopteryx* was related to small dinosaurs. If they are right, then all birds are related to the dinosaurs.

Giant Tooth

YOU WILL NEED:
- air-hardening modeling clay
- watercolor inks
- well-weathered stones
- tan shoe polish
- cloth

MESSY ACTIVITY

1 To copy a dinosaur tooth, model a big ball of clay into a shape similar to that shown here. Keep your hands wet while you are working.

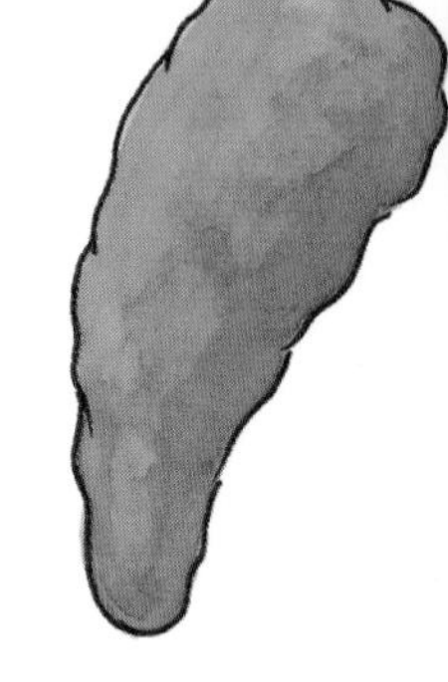

Dinosaur Teeth

Teeth make good fossils because they are hard and do not quickly disappear through decay. One of the first dinosaur fossils to be found was a jawbone with a tooth still in it. In 1824, William Buckland named the animal *Megalosaurus* ("big lizard"). Meat-eaters like *Megalosaurus* had sharp teeth, often with edges like those of a saw. A large biting tooth from the great meat-eater *Allosaurus* (right) was found to be 7 in (17 cm) long.

Plant-eaters had smaller, blunter teeth to chop and grind up their food. Some also had a beak at the front of their mouth to help them gather up and eat big mouthfuls of plants. *Iguanodon*, for example, had a narrow skull and a pointed beak.

Plant-eaters deliberately swallowed "gizzard stones," called gastroliths. These stones in the stomach helped to crush the leaves, making them easier to digest.

A duck-billed dinosaur could have as many as 700 teeth!

2 Texture the surface of the clay by pressing it against a stone or rock. Peel off the clay and mark it with stone patterns all around to give it a fossilized look.

3 Allow the clay tooth to harden. It will take a day or two.

4 Now paint the tooth using brown and ocher inks. You can apply the paint in any way that you like.

5 When the paint is dry, rub tan shoe polish into the clay to make it look shiny and weathered. The tooth makes a good paperweight.

Homemade Apatosaurus

MESSY ACTIVITY

YOU WILL NEED:
✔large plastic bottle ✔paper towel tube ✔4 toilet paper tubes ✔pencil ✔ruler ✔oak tag ✔colored tissue paper ✔scissors ✔parcel tape ✔2 buttons ✔fungicide-free wallpaper paste ✔varnish ✔glue brush ✔newspaper

1 Assemble the body of your *Apatosaurus* first. Cut two toilet paper tubes in half to make the legs. Tape the legs to the bottle with parcel tape.

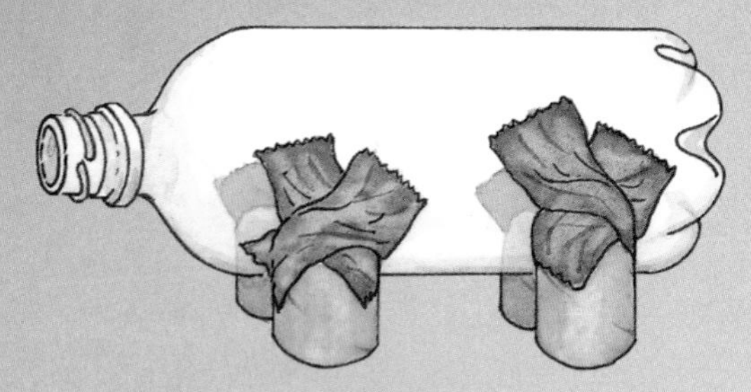

2 Make the long neck and the small head by cutting a toilet paper tube in half and cutting a segment out of each side. Tape the toilet paper tube to a paper towel tube and attach it to the top of the bottle with more parcel tape.

3 For the tail, draw around a saucer onto some oak tag and cut out the circle. Cut out a section from the circle, roll it into a cone, and fasten the edges. Stick the cone into the remaining half-tube and then tape the tail to the bottom of the bottle.

4 Tear some newspaper into thin strips (about 2 in [5 cm] wide). Mix up the paste as instructed on the package, and coat each strip of paper with it. Cover the model with at least four layers of paste-coated paper.

Plant-eaters

Apatosaurus ("headless lizard") was an enormous long-necked plant-eater. It was over 65 ft (20 m) long and weighed about 30 tons. It used its long neck to reach the treetops, where it gathered leaves to eat.

It had a very small head, which accounts for its name. It had long, delicate teeth, which may mean that it spent a lot of time in lakes and rivers, feeding on tender water plants. Its tail was very long and was whiplike at the end.

Scientists used to call it *Brontosaurus* until they realized that *Brontosaurus* fossils were the same as *Apatosaurus*. Since one dinosaur cannot have two different names, *Apatosaurus* was chosen.

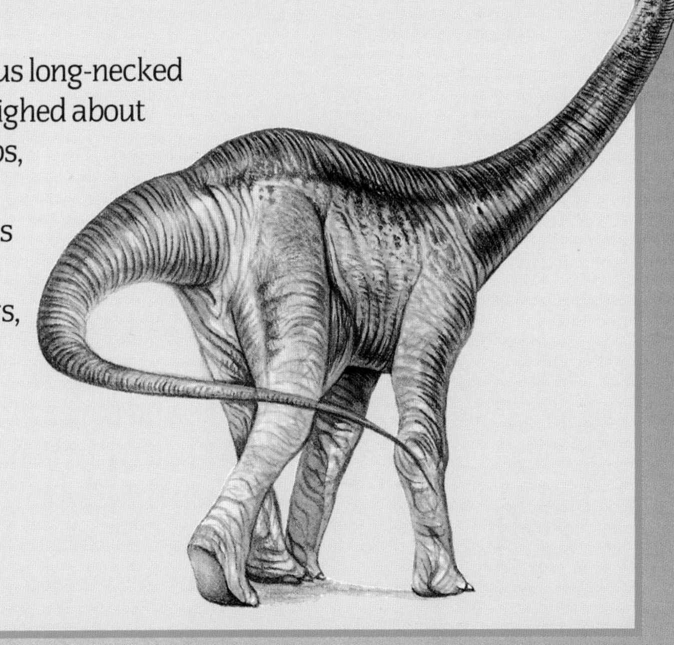

5 Now take whole sheets of colored tissue paper and soak them in paste. Wrap the wet tissue around the paper model and the legs. You can work the tissue with your fingers to make dips in the spine and shape the head.

6 When your *Apatosaurus* is dry, glue on two button eyes and varnish the whole model.

Imagine what the real *Apatosaurus* was like at over 65 ft (20 m) long!

Nest Eggs

YOU WILL NEED:
- ✓*newspaper*
- ✓*PVA glue*
- ✓*poster paint*
- ✓*air-hardening modeling clay*
- ✓*leaves*
- ✓*ruler*
- ✓*brown and yellow tissue paper*
- ✓*water*
- ✓*large round ice-cream or margarine tub*

1 To make big dinosaur eggs, scrunch a double sheet of newspaper into a ball. Scrunch it up very tightly.

2 Make several pats of clay and cover the paper ball with them. Moisten the joints and smear them together.

3 Beat the ball into an egg shape with a ruler. This will make the egg smooth and strong.

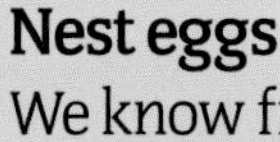

Nest eggs

We know from fossils that dinosaurs laid shelled eggs on land. Fossilized eggs and young *Protoceratops* fossils have been found in the Gobi desert in Mongolia. The eggs were over 6 in (15 cm) long. These large eggs were protected from drying out by their tough, waterproof shell. Safe inside the shell, the young dinosaur was nourished by a large supply of yolk, until it was ready to hatch out.

It is believed that dinosaurs often laid their eggs in the sand or in mud nests on high ground, away from water.

4 Make some smaller eggs in the same way, and let them dry.

5 You can paint the eggs different colors with patterns of your own choice, as we don't know what markings dinosaur eggs had.

6 The eggs need a nest. Scrunch small pieces of tissue paper into balls. Stick them all over the outside of a large round tub.

7 Make a cushion of tissue paper in your nest and put the eggs in. Cover them up with leaves just in case an egg-eating dinosaur, such as an *Oviraptor*, is on the lookout for a snack.

Oviraptor means "egg-thief."

Catch a Diplodocus

1 For this game, cut one side off a cereal box to make a tray. Tape the open end to seal it up. Strengthen all the corners with tape.

YOU WILL NEED:
✔empty cereal box ✔straws ✔scissors ✔felt-tip pens ✔glue stick ✔large plastic dishwashing liquid bottle ✔white oak tag ✔stapler ✔tape ✔corrugated paper

2 Cut a strip of corrugated paper to fit the sides of the tray—with the lines running vertically. Staple or glue the corrugated paper strip around the outside rim of the tray. Add some vegetation inside the tray.

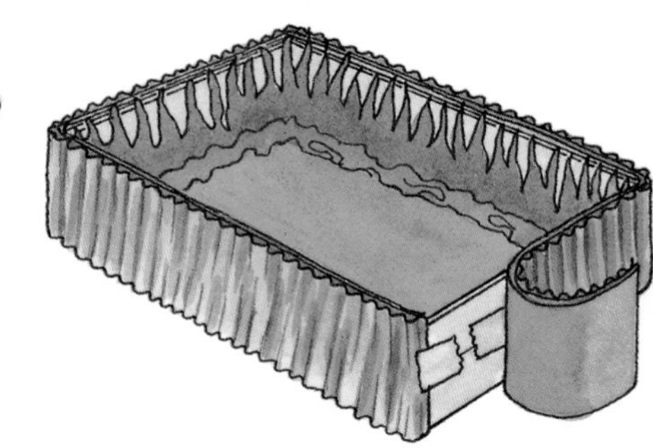

3 Copy or trace this *Diplodocus* onto oak tag. Make sure it has a long neck to fit around a straw. Draw, color, and cut out five *Diplodocus* heads.

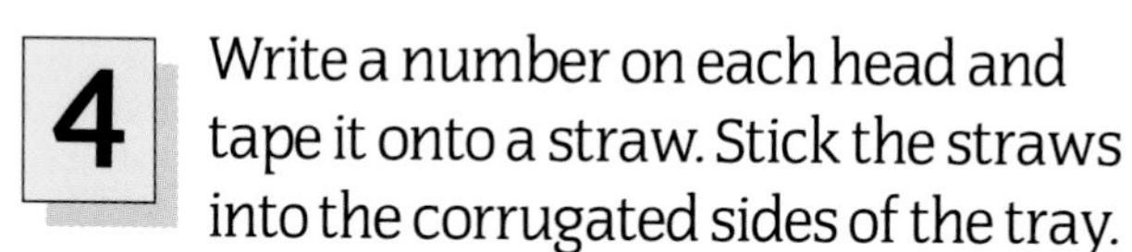

4 Write a number on each head and tape it onto a straw. Stick the straws into the corrugated sides of the tray.

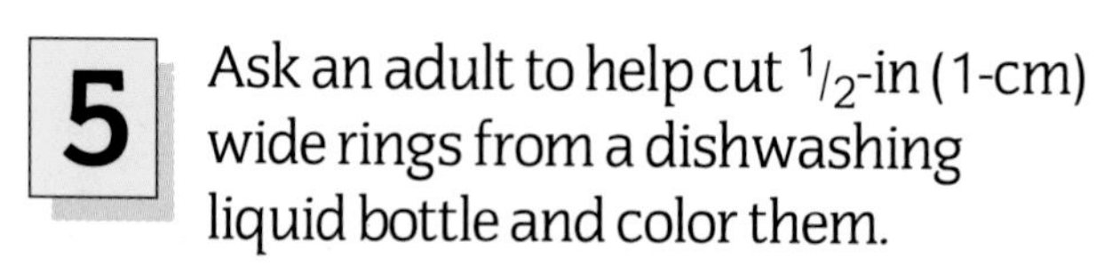

5 Ask an adult to help cut $^{1}/_{2}$-in (1-cm) wide rings from a dishwashing liquid bottle and color them.

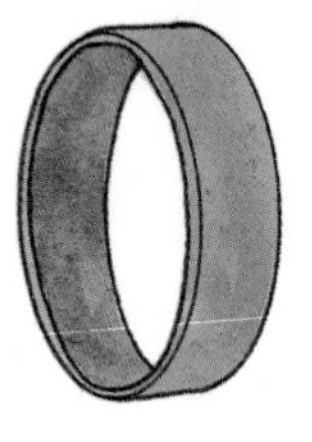

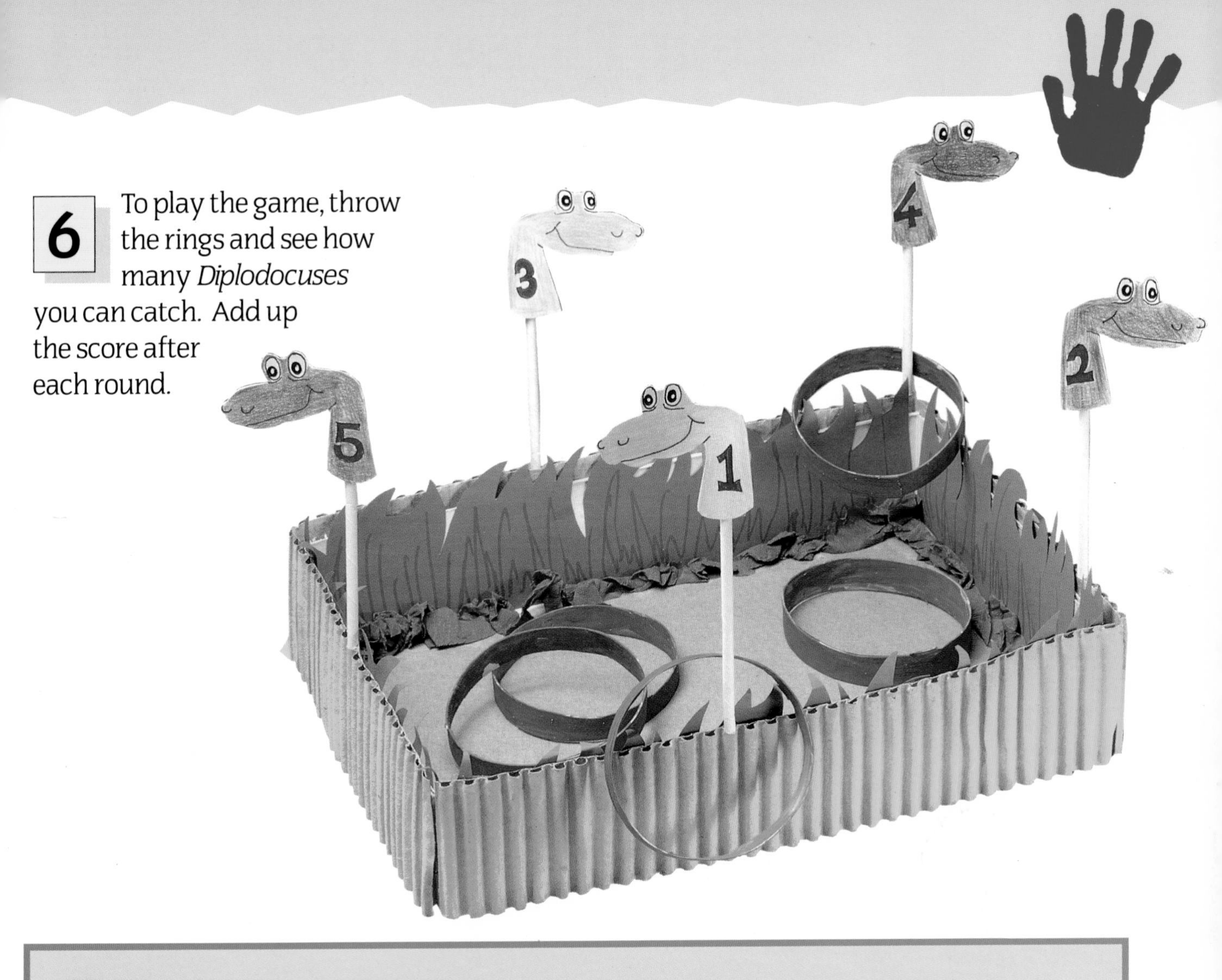

6 To play the game, throw the rings and see how many *Diplodocuses* you can catch. Add up the score after each round.

Diplodocus

Diplodocus (below left) was one of the longest land animals ever known. It was about 88 ft (27 m) long–about as long as eight cars parked end to end! Most of its length was made up by its thin neck and tail. It weighed about 10 tons and so was not one of the heaviest dinosaurs.

Its name means "double beam." This comes from the two bony skids that protected its tail as it was dragged along the ground.

Diplodocus was a plant-eater, and scientists used to think that it lived in lakes and swamps. But this is now believed to be unlikely, because it had small feet compared with its body. It would have found it difficult to walk on swampy ground without sinking in. Today it is thought that *Diplodocus* lived on land, using its long neck to reach leaves in the tops of tall trees.

Pop-up Pliosaurus

YOU WILL NEED
✔oak tag ✔scissors
✔masking tape
✔thick white cardboard 12 x 10 in (30 x 25 cm)
✔felt-tip pens ✔pencil ✔tape
✔ruler ✔tracing paper

1 Fold the cardboard in half.

2 With tracing paper and a pencil, trace the *Pliosaurus* mouth, sharp teeth, and tabs, and cut out the shape.

3 Fold a piece of oak tag–it must be big enough for the length and width of the tracing to fit on. Now place the tracing paper mouth along the fold and draw around it. This will be one jaw.

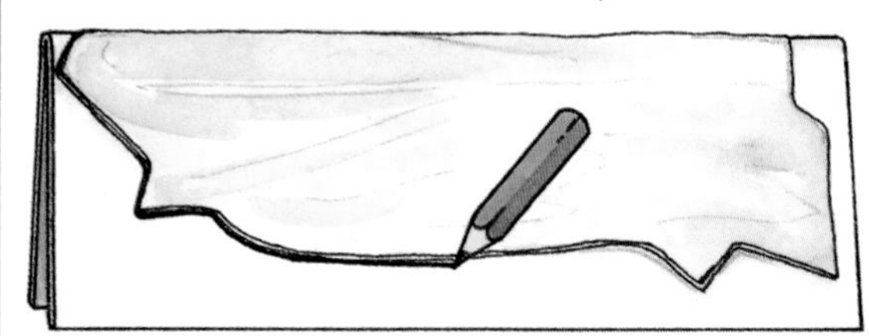

4 Make the other jaw in the same way on another piece of thin card. You now have two identical jaws.

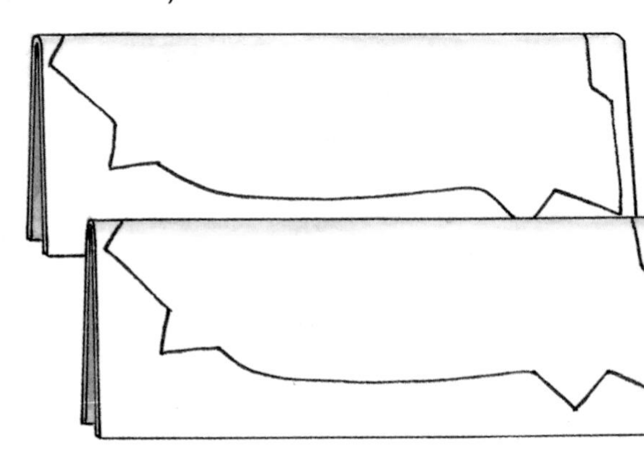

Sea Reptiles

None of the dinosaurs may actually have lived in the sea. But many large sea reptiles did exist in the Age of Reptiles. Plesiosaurs looked rather like dinosaurs. They had long necks but their bodies were round, and had paddle-like flippers. They probably fed on fish, which they snapped up with their sharp pointed teeth.

Pliosaurs were short-necked plesiosaurs and were very big–the whales of the prehistoric seas.

Ichthyosaurs ("fish lizards") were up to 40 ft (12 m) long and looked similar to the dolphins of today. Like dolphins, they came to the surface to breathe, and they also gave birth to live young in the water. Lurking in rivers and coastal waters were early crocodiles, ready to snap at any unwary animals that came within range of their large jaws.

5 Cut out the jaws–but don't cut the fold–and open them out. Then color them in–green outside and red inside.

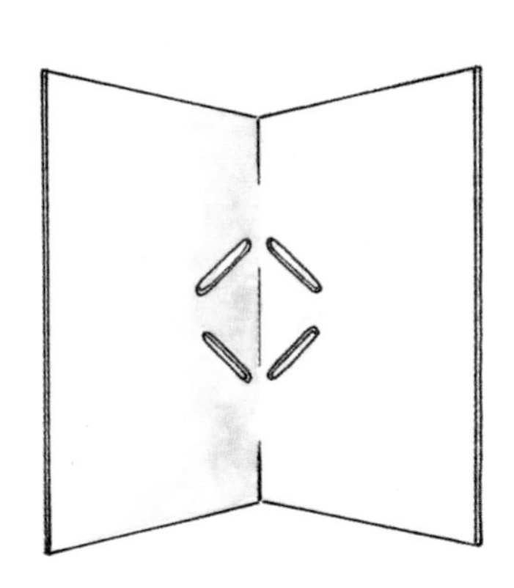

6 Ask an adult to cut four slits into the piece of thick cardboard. The cuts start $^1/_4$ inch from the center fold of the cardboard. The gap between the jaws should be no larger than 2 in (5 cm) to allow the jaws to close properly.

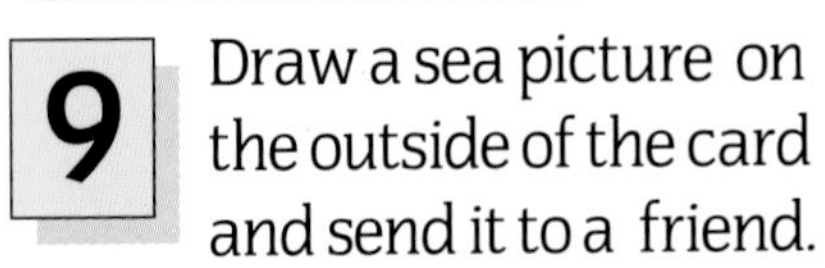

7 Before putting the tabs through the slits, fold each jaw in half. Then open it up a little and push the tabs through the slits. Open and close the card to check that it works. You might have to adjust the tabs slightly before securing them with tape on the front and back of the card.

8 Now draw eyes, fins, and a tail on the card to complete your pop-up *Pliosaurus*.

9 Draw a sea picture on the outside of the card and send it to a friend.

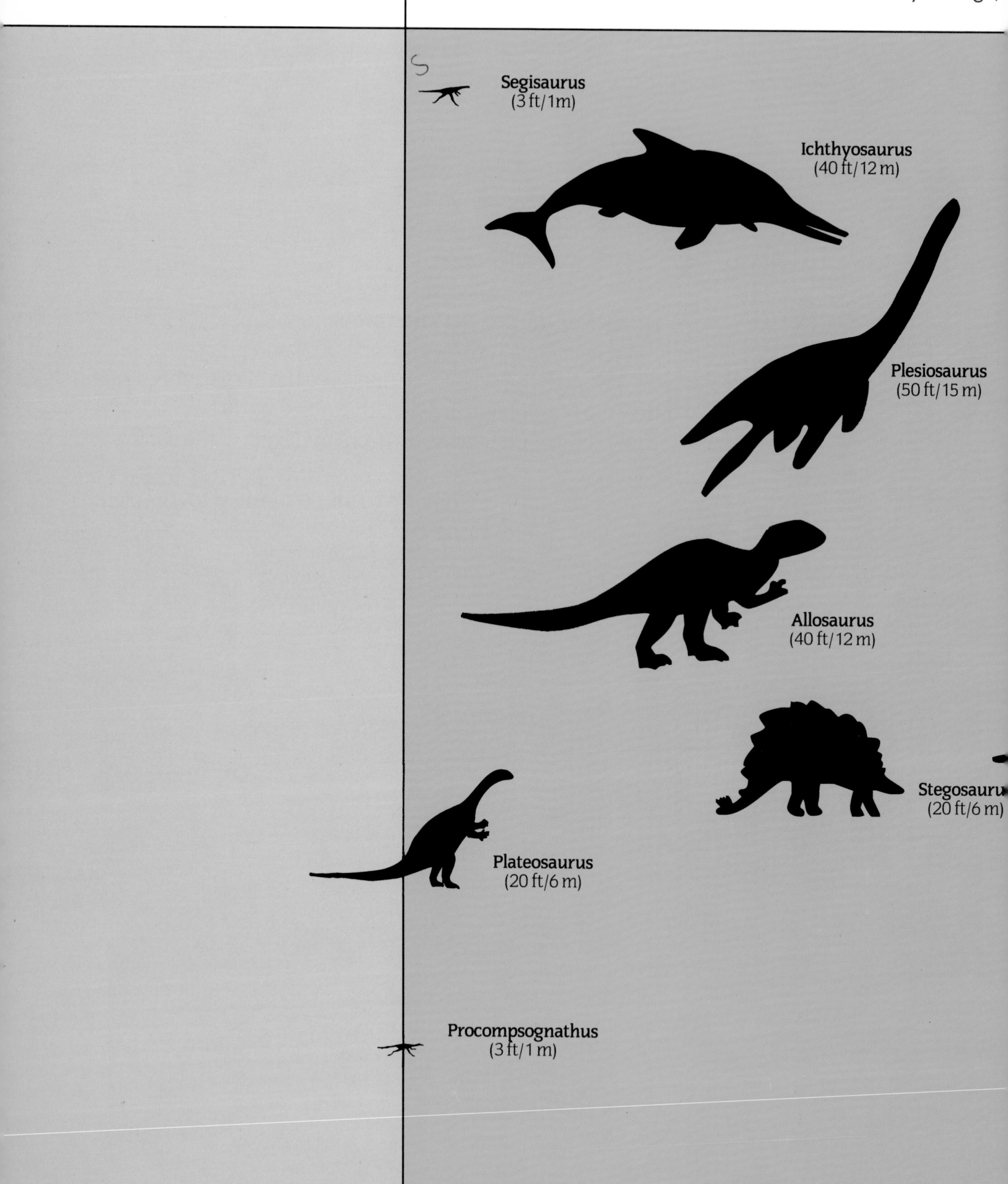
TRIASSIC PERIOD
(248 - 213 million years ago)
JURASSIC PERIOD
(213 - 144 million years ago)
Segisaurus
(3 ft/1m)
Ichthyosaurus
(40 ft/12 m)
Plesiosaurus
(50 ft/15 m)
Allosaurus
(40 ft/12 m)
Stegosauru
(20 ft/6 m)
Plateosaurus
(20 ft/6 m)
Procompsognathus
(3 ft/1 m)

CRETACEOUS PERIOD
(144 - 65 million years ago)

The end of the dinosaurs

All dinosaurs died out about 65 million years ago. It is not known definitely why this happened, but there are a lot of theories. It is thought that a huge meteorite crashed into earth and sent up a thick cloud of dust. This may have blocked out the sun's warmth, and the dinosaurs may have frozen to death.

Glossary

amphibian - an animal that can live both on land and in water, such as a frog.

continent - one of the earth's large land masses.

Cretaceous period - the third and last part of the Mesozoic era, from 140 to 65 million years ago. Dinosaurs died out at the end of this period.

dinosaur - an extinct form of reptile that lived on Earth for 165 million years.

fossil - the remains of animals or plants preserved in rocks. They include bones, teeth, and footprints.

hatch - to emerge from an egg.

ichthyosaur - a sea reptile related to the dinosaurs. It was similar to the dolphin of today.

iguana - a large South American lizard.

Jurassic period - the second part of the Mesozoic era, from 195 to 140 million years ago, when dinosaurs flourished.

mammal - a warm-blooded backboned animal whose young feed on their mother's milk.

Mesozoic era - "middle life"–the third of the four main lengths of time that we use to divide up the earth's history. It lasted from 240 to 65 million years ago and is divided into three periods–the Triassic, Jurassic, and Cretaceous.

meteorite - a lump of rock or metal that falls to Earth from outer space.

plesiosaur - a sea reptile related to the dinosaurs that swam with flippers.

pliosaur - a very big, short-necked plesiosaur.

prey - an animal hunted by another for food.

pterosaur - a winged reptile related to the dinosaurs.

reptile - a cold-blooded backboned animal, such as snakes, lizards, and crocodiles. Dinosaurs were reptiles.

skeleton - the hard framework of bones that supports and protects the soft parts of an animal's body.

skull - the bony skeleton of the head.

swamp - ground that is always wet and usually overgrown with plants and trees.

theory - an idea about something, such as a scientist's idea about what happened and why.

Triassic period - the first part of the Mesozoic era, from 240 to 195 million years ago, when dinosaurs first appeared.

yolk - the part of an egg that nourishes the developing young animal.

Resources

Books to read

Digging Up Dinosaurs
by Aliki
(New York: HarperTrophy, 1988)

The Kingfisher Illustrated Dinosaur Encyclopedia
by David Burnie
(New York: Kingfisher, 2001)

Dinosaur Dinners
by Sharon Cosner
(New York: Franklin Watts, 1991)

How To Draw Dinosaurs
by Michael Laplaca
(New York: Scholastic, 2004)

All The Dirt On Dinosaurs
by Don Lessem
(New York: Torkids, 2001)

Eyewitness: Dinosaur
by David Norman and Angela Milner
(New York: Dorling Kindersley, 2000)

Dinosaurs (Magic Tree House Research Guide)
by Will And Ma Osborne
(New York: Random House Books for Young Readers, 2000)

Big Book of Dinosaurs
by Robert Walters (Illustrator), Donald F. Glut, Gillian King,
(Philadelphia: Courage Books, 2001)

Pocket Factfiles Dinosaurs
by Adam Ward
(New York: Sterling, 2003)

Places to visit

American Museum of Natural History
Central Park West at 79th Street
New York, New York
(212) 769-5100
Website: www.amnh.org

Carnegie Museum
4400 Forbes Avenue
Pittsburgh, PA 15213
(412) 622-3131
email: cmnhweb@CarnegieMNH.org
Website: http://www.carnegiemnh.org/

Dinosaur National Monument
Dinosaur QuarryVisitor Center
Jensen, Utah
(435) 789-2115
Website: www.cr.nps.gov/museum/exhibits/dino/overview.html

Page Museum
La Brea Tar Pits
5801 Wilshire Blvd.
Los Angeles, CA 90036
(323) 934-PAGE (7243)
Email: info@tarpits.org
Website: www.tarpits.org/

Natural History Museum of Los Angeles County
900 Exposition Boulevard
Los Angeles, CA 90007
(213) 763-DINO (3466)
Email: info@nhm.org
Website: www.nhm.org/

Royal Ontario Museum...
100 Queen's Park
Toronto, Ontario M5S 2C6
Canada
(416) 586-5549
Website: www.rom.on.ca/

Smithsonian National Museum of Natural History
10th Street and Constitution Ave., NW
Washington, D.C. 20560
(202) 633-1000
Email: info@si.edu .
Website: www.mnh.si.edu/

Index

Additional photographs:
The Natural History Museum, London 15(tr), 25(b); Pat Morris 11(l), 17(b), 18(l), 22(bl).